Table of
CONTENTS

- Understanding the Meaning of Self-Care

- Breaking it Down

- Physical Self-Care

- Taking Care of Emotions

- Our Social Needs

- Work-Life Balance

- Making Our Environment Work for Us

- Managing Finances

- Spiritual Self-Care

- Build in Joy

Understanding the Meaning
SELF-CARE

HELLO,

I know the world of mental health and self-care can be so hard to navigate. It can feel so daunting to organize your personal self-care journey. This workbook is filled with guides, activities, information, and opportunities to reflect. We wanted this workbook to be interactive, helpful, and most of all, personal.

Everyone's experience taking care of themselves is so different! Each of our lives and individual perspectives will shape the way we need self-care practices. Use what you need and disregard the rest. We love to inspire self-awareness and help you cultivate self-care. Whether it's through this comprehensive workbook, or simple posts on instagram. Find what fuels you!

Best regards,

Selfcare.Recipe

Breaking it Down
SELF-CARE

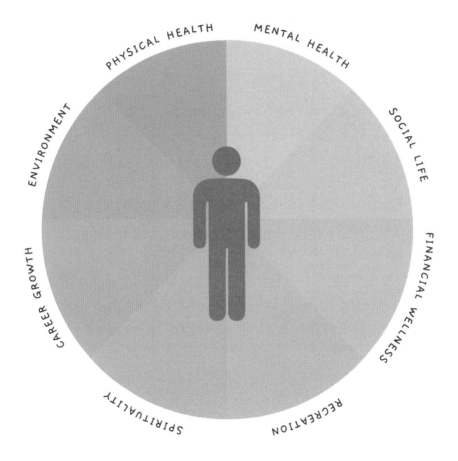

PHYSICAL HEALTH · MENTAL HEALTH · SOCIAL LIFE · ENVIRONMENT · FINANCIAL WELLNESS · CAREER GROWTH · SPIRITUALITY · RECREATION

Life is one big balancing act. Let's be honest, it is impossible to do it all and "perfect" self-care. BUT we can use this guide to improve ourselves and our lives through reminders in each area of life!

Physical
SELF-CARE

Physical health and emotional health are intimately intertwined in what's known as the mind-body connection. The mind-body connection dictates a lot of how we feel, how we show up, and ultimately our quality of life! If you are feeling a bit disconnected, practices such as progressive muscle relaxation, stress reduction, meditation, mindfulness, and yoga, are just a few ways to strengthen the mind-body connection.

Examples of this connection can be seen in our body's reaction to stress, relationships, exercise, food, and sleep. Chronic stress affects the body in a negative way, and over long periods of time, long-term stress can make us more susceptible to diabetes, hypertension, heart diseases, and some infections. The mind-body connection can also be incredibly positive, whether it is endorphins produced after exercise, stress relief during a massage, or the happy chemicals released when we connect to our loved ones.

Self-Care
QUIZ

Answer the questions with Yes/No and see if you have been taking a good care of yourself through the number of yes in your answers!

I get enough sleep (aiming for 7-9 hours of quality restful sleep each night)

I drink an adequate amount of water

I consume various fruits, vegetables, whole grains, and lean proteins

I feel in tune with my body and what it needs

I try to get my body moving each day (in any way that works for me)

I have a bedtime routine

I practice relaxation techniques regularly

I prioritize personal hygiene each day

I feel happy and healthy

$\frac{20}{12}{22}$ Planner BEDTIME

During sleep, your body is working to support healthy brain function and maintain your physical health. Sleep plays an enormous role in maintaining our serotonin levels. Serotonin's primary action in the body is to sedate, therefore, it is closely tied to how energy is — or is not — expended (i.e. exercise and sleep). Without sleep, our brains can be negatively affected, by messing with our brain's response to serotonin.

BED CHECKLIST

EXAMPLE

READ 20 PAGES

SKINCARE

MEDITATION

FINISH THE PODCAST EPISODE

WATCH A TV SHOW

JOURNALING

MY ROUTINE

1.

2.

3.

4.

HABIT TRACKER

Date _____

MOOD:

WATER TRACKING:

WHAT KIND OF MOVEMENT DO YOU ENJOY?

1.

2.

3.

 Challenge: Try to move your body each day this week! Keep track of your progress...

DID YOU MOVE TODAY?

M T W T F S S

LET YOURSELF REST AND RECHARGE. GIVE YOURSELF PERMISSION TO LAY IN BED ALL DAY. TAKE ON THE NEXT DAY WITH YOUR BATTERY FULL.

Emotional
SELF-CARE

Bubble baths, massages, lighting candles, or grabbing a treat are all excellent ways to show ourselves a bit of extra love. These things will surely make you feel relaxed, but sometimes what we really need runs deeper than this. Taking care of your emotions requires a lot of self-awareness and hard work to reach deep rooted health. Feelings contribute to long-term health outcomes and overall life satisfaction.

It may be appealing to suppress, ignore, or disregard our emotions, but emotions demand to be felt. According to Harvard brain scientist Dr. Jill Bolte Taylor, ninety seconds is all it takes to identify an emotion and allow it to pass. When we honor our emotions by pausing for only ninety seconds and labeling what we are feeling, it calms our brain and allows it to move on without dwelling on negative emotion. Do not let temporary comfort steal your authenticity and peace.

Self-Care
QUIZ

Answer the questions with Yes/No and see if you have been taking good care of yourself through the number of times you answer yes!

I know which activities make me feel recharged

I can easily label my emotions

I let myself cry when I need too

I frequently check in with myself throughout the day

I rest when I need it

I communicate my feelings without feeling shame or embarrassment

I speak kindly to myself and others

I always make time for myself to slow down

I feel capable of coping with my emotions

DO A RELAXING BODY SCAN

FIND SOMEWHERE TO SIT OR LAY DOWN COMFORTABLY. START AT THE TOP OF YOUR HEAD AND MAKE YOUR WAY DOWN THE BODY. SQUEEZE EACH MUSCLE FOR TEN SECONDS, THEN RELEASE. ANSWER THESE QUESTIONS AS YOU GO TO GET IN TOUCH WITH YOUR BODY.

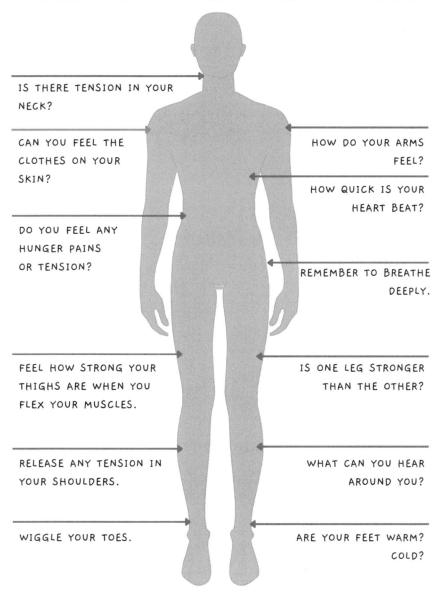

IS THERE TENSION IN YOUR NECK?

CAN YOU FEEL THE CLOTHES ON YOUR SKIN?

DO YOU FEEL ANY HUNGER PAINS OR TENSION?

HOW DO YOUR ARMS FEEL?

HOW QUICK IS YOUR HEART BEAT?

REMEMBER TO BREATHE DEEPLY.

FEEL HOW STRONG YOUR THIGHS ARE WHEN YOU FLEX YOUR MUSCLES.

IS ONE LEG STRONGER THAN THE OTHER?

RELEASE ANY TENSION IN YOUR SHOULDERS.

WHAT CAN YOU HEAR AROUND YOU?

WIGGLE YOUR TOES.

ARE YOUR FEET WARM? COLD?

MINI MENTAL HEALTH CHALLENGE

Drink lots of water today!

Get your body moving

Talk to or text someone you love

Smell something comforting

Tidy up your bedroom, take those cups to the sink

Do that thing you have been avoiding

Eat a happy safe food

Go to bed early, put down that phone!

Look in the mirror and find three things you like

YOU CAN DO IT!!

YOU HAVEN'T LIVED
YOUR HAPPIEST MOST
CHERISHED MEMORY
YET. THE BEST DAYS
ARE YET TO COME.

Social
SELF-CARE

Social self-care is how we interact with our community and show up in relationships. When we have family, friends, co-workers, partners, or children, our day may seem packed full of socializing! But, if we simply go through the motions without truly connecting with our people, the relationships we hold dear can fizzle and no one will be getting their social needs met. Everyone needs a strong network to show up during good and bad times.

We as humans are wired for connection. Be sure to check in with yourself about how you are showing up in your relationships and how they are showing up for you! If we become aware of what kind of socializing drains our battery and who energizes us when spending time together, it can free up space for quality relationships and make socializing more enjoyable. Put down your phone, get a babysitter, schedule in the time face to face, make a surprise phone call, or have that hard conversation!

Self-Care
QUIZ

Answer the questions with Yes/No and see if you have been taking a good care of yourself through the number of times you answer yes!

I have friends and family that I enjoy being around

I can trust my circle to be there for me in hard times

I know when my social battery is drained

My community celebrates good news with me

I look forward to holidays and social activities

I have people in my life that give me honest feedback

I feel comfortable setting boundaries with loved ones

I make time for friends and family

People in my life reciprocate effort

IT'S NOT YOUR JOB TO BE EVERYTHING FOR EVERYONE.

Professional
SELF-CARE

Writer Annie Dillard famously said, "How we spend our days is, of course, how we spend our lives." For many of us, a large portion of our day is spent at work; in fact, the average person will spend 90,000 hours at work over a lifetime. If you let it, work can consume a large chunk of your life. If you are someone who is fulfilled and devoted to your career, that is incredible! If your job just pays the bills and is not a priority, that is great too!

If you are a parent or caretaker and your work is keeping humans alive with few breaks, amazing! This workbook is not an excuse to beat yourself up or guilt you into exhausting yourself by doing it all. Wherever you are, adjust where you can. Work is a necessity that is inescapable, often times taking up a lot of our energy and time. As long as you take time to reflect and make changes when you need it. We are all doing the best we can!

Self-Care
QUIZ

Answer the questions with Yes/No and see if you have been taking a good care of yourself through the number of times you answer yes!

I don't dread going to work on Monday

I set boundaries for the work I agree to do

I don't stress about work in my free time

I have a routine that works for me when getting ready for work

I know I am a valuable asset

I have a routine that works for me to decompress returning from work

I know the symptoms of burn out

I don't say yes to things I do not have the capacity for

My work aligns with my values

Don't set
yourself
on FIRE
to keep others
WARM

Work-Life Balance
TIPS

Ideally we would love our jobs and enjoy every minute, but this is not often the reality. Learning to set boundaries and prioritize what matters most to you is life changing!

Use time saving ways to do things. Time is precious. If you can find the shortcuts to the daily activity that you're doing to save some time, it will pay off in the long run!

Build successful relationships with coworkers and supervisors so you can have the support you need to set boundaries and take time off. Communicate what you need!

Don't over stay your time at a job because you are comfortable. If the position is not fulfilling your needs and optimizing your life. Find another!

Stop wasting time on unnecessary things. Manage your time well so you will not ruin your productivity at work.

Schedule in time for the things that matter. Family time, intimacy, and self-care should all be built into your day. This is how you prioritize balance.

Accept imperfection. There is not a perfect way to create balance in your life and you do not need to be at 100% at work every day.

Don't be afraid to unplug. Don't check your email when clocked out. Leave your work phone in the car. Anything that creates boundaries with yourself.

Environmental
SELF-CARE

How does your environment make you feel? Are you stressed using your office at work? Do you feel relaxed in your sleep space? Environmental self-care encourages you to cultivate spaces that are functional and positive. This will be different for everyone! Do you feel energized or overwhelmed by bright colors? Do you feel comforted by having stuff around or disorganized? Make sure you are making your environment your own.

Sometimes life gets busy and we do not notice how the outside effects the inside. This does not mean you need to redecorate your home, or buy many candles you don't need, but make small changes and monitor your habits to make sure your environment is working for you. Keeping yourself organized and comfortable can improve your sleep, relaxation time, and relationships.

Self-Care
QUIZ

Answer the questions with Yes/No and see if you have been taking a good care of yourself through the number of times you answer yes!

I have somewhere to hang out that is not work or home

I have safe people around me

I monitor my phone and screen use

I make my space my own with decor and things that bring me joy

I maintain habits to keep my space organized and clean

I get fresh air frequently

My work space caters to my needs

I listen to music that I like often

I pay attention to the way my environment makes me feel

Improving your Environment

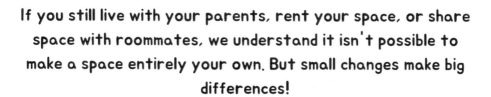

TIPS

If you still live with your parents, rent your space, or share space with roommates, we understand it isn't possible to make a space entirely your own. But small changes make big differences!

If you have a hard time folding or hanging your laundry, it always ends up staying on that chair in your room or never leaves the hamper. Why not put clothing away in bins?

If you are frequently stressed and anxious, adjust where you decompress. Use cozy blankets and dim lighting.

Organize your desk for work. Add in systems that help you be productive. If you constantly have to bring jackets to keep warm, buy yourself a space heater!

Start decluttering your closet and junk drawers every few months. Donate extra clothing locally and buy clothing that fits that you feel confident in!

Buy an extra candle for your bathroom or air freshener for your car. You will be surprised how you perk up when your space smells nice.

Rearrange your room and fill the walls with artwork that sparks joy, or pictures of loved ones with good memories. Deep clean while you are at it!

Buy a plant or freshen up your garden. If you don't enjoy plants in your space, get outside and enjoy the outdoors!

Financial
SELF-CARE

Financial worries are a major cause for stress in our lives. Especially for those of us that are still figuring it all out. Devoting our time and energy to secure a plan and mindset for our finances is financial self-care. Talking about money and thinking about money can be so daunting that we just procrastinate and keep our fingers crossed that it all works out, but this is going to produce more stress in the long run.

In this day and age there are so many resources that can help us reach our financial goals, and keep the pressure of finances to a minimum. Whether it is free Youtube courses, budgeting apps, spreadsheets, or support groups, money is hard to manage but it can also empower us to live a fulfilling life that aligns with our values. If we are able to budget for self-care, joy, and stress reduction, then it is more likely that we practice them in our daily lives!

Self-Care
QUIZ

Answer the questions with Yes/No and see if you have been taking a good care of yourself through the number of times you answer yes!

I have financial goals

I track how much I make and how much I spend

I don't spend money on things that are not in my budget

I have a savings account that I move funds to frequently

I know my credit score

I don't feel obligated to monetize my hobbies

I understand I don't need to be productive all the time

I feel comfortable talking about money

I set boundaries for myself about spending

30 DAY
Financial Health Challenge

DAY 1	DAY 2	DAY 3	DAY 4	DAY 5
Make a list of your assets and liabilities	Calculate your net worth	List the things that are categorized as a 'need'	List the things that are categorized as a 'want'	No spend day
DAY 6	**DAY 7**	**DAY 8**	**DAY 9**	**DAY 10**
Review last month's bank statement	Unsubscribe from unused services	Check your energy efficiency and adjust	Download a budgeting app or tool	Create a rough outline of monthly expenses
DAY 11	**DAY 12**	**DAY 13**	**DAY 14**	**DAY 15**
Calculate boundaries on 'needs' & 'wants'	No spend day	Write a list of short-term financial goals	Write a list of long-term financial goals	Reflect on your relationship with spending
DAY 16	**DAY 17**	**DAY 18**	**DAY 19**	**DAY 20**
Pause & think for 1 minute before a purchase	Research common financial terms	Ask a trusted source about their financial planning	Finalize a personal budget	Listen to a podcast about finance
DAY 21	**DAY 22**	**DAY 23**	**DAY 24**	**DAY 25**
Research credit card options	Check your credit score	Find one way to improve your credit score	Brainstorm one thing that can be cut from your budget	No spend day
DAY 26	**DAY 27**	**DAY 28**	**DAY 29**	**DAY 30**
Decide how much will go to savings each month	Look into different saving accounts pros & cons	Talk with someone about your finances & progress	Buy yourself something nice	Congratulate yourself on your hard work!

Monthly Budget

Income			Expenses	
Income-1			Month	
Income-2				
Other Income			Budget	
	Total Income			

Bill To Be Paid	Due Date	Amount	Paid	Notes
	Total			

Monthly Summary

Total Income	Total Expenses	Difference

Notes

Spiritual
SELF-CARE

I know that spirituality is a deeply personal experience. It can come in so many shapes and sizes, as it should! Anything that helps develop your understanding of the world and cultivate a deeper meaning and purpose is spiritual self-care. If you are still struggling to develop practices that ring true to you, let's try something new. Or if you already have things important to your spiritual journey let's do more of it!

Spiritual practices should develop your ability to self-reflect, promote understanding and create meaning for life events, shape personal values, and align with how you interact with and care for others. Habits such as meditation, being in nature, mindfulness, yoga, gratitude, prayer, walks, manifesting, and meeting with community can really establish and maintain connection to spirituality. Let this be a reminder to do more of what makes you most connected!

Self-Care

QUIZ

Answer the questions with Yes/No and see if you have been taking a good care of yourself through the number of times you answer yes!

I think about the meaning of life

I frequently connect with myself or a higher power

I pause to remind myself that life is bigger than me

I often put down my phone and other distractions and let myself just be

I don't find it challenging to self reflect and be alone with my thoughts

I try to be mindful of my experiences in my daily life

I am open to other perspectives

I frequently connect with others that share similar beliefs to me

I have loved ones I can ask questions to and share my experience with

I am GRATEFUL for...

 Challenge: Name three things you are grateful for each day of the week. Track your progress!

WHAT ARE YOU THANKFUL FOR TODAY?

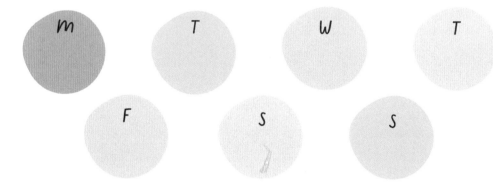

m   T   W   T

F   S   S

MY FAVOURITE QUOTES:

Challenge: Find quotes that resonate with your spiritual journey! Write them here.

66   66   66

Reflection

_____
_____
_____
_____
_____
_____
_____
_____
_____
_____
_____
_____
_____
_____
_____
_____
_____
_____

NEVER
forget that...

You can mistakes, it's a part of life

We are all a work in progress

You deserve unconditional love

The world is better with you in it

You are stronger than you know

Asking for help is a sign of strength

Focus on what you can control

Recreational
SELF-CARE

Recreational self-care is a vital pillar in a fulfilling life. It is simply making time for fun and scheduling it into your day. I know that we all have a long running to-do list. This keeps our life running smoothly and sometimes we prioritize productivity because we need to. But if we notice this happens often, it's a habit. When we prioritize happy activities it often benefits our productivity levels and our relationships.

This is an opportunity to connect with your inner child and bring the spark back to your experience. Step away from your agenda and and lean into what doesn't have expectations of us. This might feel challenging for some, especially in those hard phases of life. This can look like grabbing coffee on the way to pick up groceries, playing piano when the kids do, playing good music driving to work, or going on a walk during your lunch break. Find ways to build in joy wherever you can!

Self-Care
QUIZ

Answer the questions with Yes/No and see if you have been taking a good care of yourself through the number of times you answer yes!

I know which activities bring me joy

I devote enough time towards fun

I am open to trying new things

I schedule time for me to do the things that I enjoy frequently

I say yes to things that sound fun for me

My loved ones want to do fun things with me, and I want to do fun things with them

I am able to leave my to-do list alone when it is time to enjoy the day

I am not experiencing symptoms of extreme burn out

I look forward to free time

Recreational
ACTIVITY IDEAS

Try out karaoke and sing your lungs out.	Pack up a picnic and spend a day at the park.	Bundle up and go star gazing.	Buy some crayons and doodle or color.
Head to an arcade and play all the games.	Take a pottery or painting class. (even online)	Head to a local aquarium or museum.	Bake something while listening to a favorite album.
Learn an instrument; ukulele, guitar, or drums?	Get on Pinterest, make a bucket list.	Build a LEGO set or puzzle.	Play an old card or board game you love.
Go out to a trampoline park, get in the foam pit!	Make a pillow fort to watch a movie.	Go to a comedy show or concert you like!	Try out a new hobby you have always been interested in.
Do a dance work out, learn a routine.	Run through the sprinklers and lay in the sun.	Do some chalk art near your home!	Read a book on the floor with a favorite snack!

ACTIVITIES PLANNER

Date: _____

I feel the most joy when I:

ACTIVITIES I PLAN TO TRY THIS WEEK

ACTIVITY 1

ACTIVITY 2

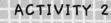

ACTIVITY 3

Reflection

_____
_____
_____
_____
_____
_____
_____
_____
_____
_____
_____
_____
_____
_____
_____
_____
_____

Made in the USA
Las Vegas, NV
03 November 2023

80183265R00024